Great Words of Our Time

GREAT WORDS

Memorable Thoughts

of Famous Men and Women

of the 20th Century

OF OUR TIME

Selected by

Dee Danner Barwick

♛ Hallmark Editions

Photograph of the Matterhorn reproduced courtesy
the Swiss National Tourist Office.
Photograph of the earth reproduced courtesy the
National Aeronautics and Space Administration.
Other photographs courtesy Black Star, Tristram
Dunn, Carter Hamilton, Shostal, and David Strout.
Excerpt by Archibald MacLeish from The New York Times
of December 25, 1968. © 1968 by The New York Times
Company. Reprinted by permission.

Great Words of Our Time

The most incomprehensible thing
about the world is that it is
comprehensible.

ALBERT EINSTEIN

To see the earth as it truly is, small and blue and beautiful in that eternal silence where it floats, is to see riders on the earth together, brothers on that bright loveliness in the eternal cold—brothers who know now they are truly brothers.

ARCHIBALD MacLEISH

I am not afraid of tomorrow, for I have seen yesterday and I love today.

WILLIAM ALLEN WHITE

Truth has no special time of its own. Its hour is now—always.

ALBERT SCHWEITZER

In every generation there has to be some fool who will speak the truth as he sees it.

BORIS PASTERNAK

5

There are as many nights as days,
and the one is just as long as the
other in the year's course. Even a
happy life cannot be without a
measure of darkness, and the
word "happy" would lose its
meaning if it were not balanced
by sadness. It is far better to take
things as they come along with
patience and equanimity.

CARL JUNG

I like trees because they seem
more resigned to the way they
have to live than other things do.

WILLA CATHER

The world will never have lasting
peace so long as men reserve for
war the finest human qualities.
Peace, no less than war, requires
idealism and self-sacrifice and
a righteous and dynamic faith.

JOHN FOSTER DULLES

When you can, always advise
people to do what you see they
really want to do, so long as what
they want to do isn't dangerously
unlawful, stupidly unsocial or
obviously impossible. Doing
what they want to do, they may
succeed; doing what they don't
want to do, they won't.
JAMES GOULD COZZENS

All of our ideas
come from the natural world:
trees equal umbrellas.
WALLACE STEVENS

Nice guys finish last.
LEO DUROCHER

It is often easier to fight for one's
principles than to live up to them.
ADLAI STEVENSON

On the stage ... masks are assumed with some regard to procedure; in everyday life, the participants act their parts without consideration either for suitability of scene or for the words spoken by the rest of the cast: the result is a general tendency for things to be brought to the level of farce even when the theme is serious enough.

ANTHONY POWELL

Life was meant to be lived and curiosity must be kept alive. One must never, for whatever reason, turn his back on life.

ELEANOR ROOSEVELT

The worst sin toward our fellow creatures is not to hate them, but to be indifferent to them; that's the essence of inhumanity.

GEORGE BERNARD SHAW

I have never quite understood
this sex symbol business, but
if I'm going to be a symbol of
something, I'd rather have it sex
than some of the other things
they've got symbols for.

MARILYN MONROE

More men are killed by
overwork than the importance
of the world justifies.

RUDYARD KIPLING

Happiness is a wine of the rarest
vintage and seems
insipid to a vulgar taste.

LOGAN PEARSALL SMITH

Love does not consist in gazing at
each other but in looking
together in the same direction.

ANTOINE DE SAINT-EXUPERY

9

Man is condemned to be free;
because once thrown into
the world, he is responsible for
everything he does.

JEAN PAUL SARTRE

Life in the twentieth century is
like a parachute jump: you have
to get it right the first time.

MARGARET MEAD

When you can do the common
things of life in an uncommon
way, you will command the
attention of the world.

GEORGE WASHINGTON CARVER

The only limit to our realization
of tomorrow will be our doubts
of today. Let us move forward
with strong and active faith.

FRANKLIN DELANO ROOSEVELT

But what is happiness except the
simple harmony between
a man and the life he leads?
ALBERT CAMUS

Everyone is a prisoner of his own
experiences. No one can
eliminate prejudices—just
recognize them.
EDWARD R. MURROW

When you reread a classic you do
not see more in the book than
you did before; you see more in
you than there was before.
CLIFTON FADIMAN

Lord, deliver me from the man
who never makes a mistake, and
also from the man who makes
the same mistake twice.
WILLIAM J. MAYO

Do not the most moving
moments of our lives find us all
without words?

MARCEL MARCEAU

Education is a social process. . . .
Education is growth. . . .
Education is not preparation for
life; education is life itself.

JOHN DEWEY

I do not want the peace which
passeth understanding, I want the
understanding which bringeth
peace.

HELEN KELLER

When the world seems large and
complex, we need to remember
that great world ideals all begin
in some home neighborhood.

KONRAD ADENAUER

We cannot learn from one
another until we stop shouting at
one another—until we speak
quietly enough so that our words
can be heard as well as our voices.
RICHARD M. NIXON

What another would have done
as well as you, do not do it.
What another would have said as
well as you, do not say it; written
as well, do not write it. Be faithful
to that which exists nowhere but
in yourself—and there make
yourself indispensable.
ANDRE GIDE

Remember always that you have
not only the right to be an
individual; you have an obligation
to be one. You cannot make any
useful contribution in life unless
you do this.
ELEANOR ROOSEVELT

Not until the creation and maintenance of decent conditions of life for all men are recognized and accepted as a common obligation of all men . . . shall we . . . be able to speak of mankind as civilized.

ALBERT EINSTEIN

It is through the idealism of youth that man catches sight of truth, and in that idealism he possesses a wealth which he must never exchange for anything else.

ALBERT SCHWEITZER

It is, of course, a trite observation to say that we live "in a period of transition." Many people have said this at many times. Adam may well have made the remark to Eve on leaving the Garden of Eden.

HAROLD MacMILLAN

A baby is God's opinion that the world should go on.

CARL SANDBURG

Peace is a daily, a weekly, a monthly process, gradually changing opinions, slowly eroding old barriers, quietly building new structures. And however undramatic the pursuit of peace, the pursuit must go on.

JOHN F. KENNEDY

Conscience is the inner voice that warns us somebody may be looking.

H. L. MENCKEN

The first thing to do in life is to do with purpose what one proposes to do.

PABLO CASALS

I believe that man will not merely
endure; he will prevail.
WILLIAM FAULKNER

Poetry ennobles the heart and the eyes, and unveils the meaning of all things upon which the heart and the eyes dwell. It discovers the secret rays of the universe, and restores to us forgotten paradises.

EDITH SITWELL

The foundations of civilization are no stronger and no more enduring than the corporate integrity of the homes on which they rest. If the home deteriorates, civilization will crumble and fall.

BILLY GRAHAM

Children not only have to learn what their parents learned in school, but also have to learn *how to learn*. This has to be recognized as a new problem which is only partly solved.

MARGARET MEAD

I don't know what your destiny
will be, but one thing I know: the
only ones among you who will
be really happy are those who
will have sought and found how
to serve.

ALBERT SCHWEITZER

All progress has resulted
from people who took unpopular
positions.

ADLAI STEVENSON

Oh, what a tangled web do
parents weave when they think
that their children are naive.

OGDEN NASH

There's an element of truth in
every idea that lasts long enough
to be called corny.

IRVING BERLIN

A friendship founded on
business is better than a business
founded on friendship.
JOHN D. ROCKEFELLER

People is all everything is, all it
has ever been, all it can ever be.
WILLIAM SAROYAN

The victor belongs to the spoils.
F. SCOTT FITZGERALD

There are two ways of spreading
light: to be the candle
or the mirror that reflects it.
EDITH WHARTON

Remember, no one can make you
feel inferior without your consent.
ELEANOR ROOSEVELT

It is the individual who knows
how little he knows about
himself who stands a reasonable
chance of finding out something
about himself before he dies.

S. I. HAYAKAWA

The reason why worry kills more
people than work is that
more people worry than work.

ROBERT FROST

You grow up the day you have
your first real laugh at yourself.

ETHEL BARRYMORE

Never look down to test the
ground before taking your next
step: only he who keeps his eye
fixed on the far horizon will find
his right road.

DAG HAMMARSKJOLD

We do not remember days,
we remember moments.
CESARE PAVESE

One of the best ways to persuade
others is with your ears—
by listening to them.

DEAN RUSK

I've never been poor, only broke.
Being poor is a frame of mind.
Being broke is only a temporary
situation.

MIKE TODD

To understand is not only to
pardon, but in the end to love.

WALTER LIPPMANN

Our strength lies, not alone in our
proving grounds and our
stockpiles, but in our ideals, our
goals, and their universal appeal
to all men who are struggling
to breathe free.

ADLAI STEVENSON

The meeting of two personalities
is like the contact of two chemical
substances: if there is any
reaction, both are transformed.

CARL JUNG

Youth is happy because it has the
ability to see beauty. Anyone who
keeps the ability to see beauty
never grows old.

FRANZ KAFKA

Injustice anywhere is a threat
to justice everywhere.

MARTIN LUTHER KING, JR.

Science has taught us how to put
the atom to work. But to make it
work for good instead of for evil
lies in the domain dealing with
the principles of human duty.

BERNARD M. BARUCH

It is very easy to forgive others
their mistakes; it takes more grit
and gumption to forgive them
for having witnessed your own.
JESSAMYN WEST

What one doesn't realize in
ordinary mental health is that
daily life is a *show*. You have to
put on a right costume, to
improvise right speeches, to do
right actions, and all this isn't
automatic, it takes concentration
and work and a simply amazing
degree of control.
HERMAN WOUK

If there is any responsibility in the
cycle of life it must be that one
generation owes to the next that
strength by which it can come to
face ultimate concerns in its own
way.
ERIK H. ERIKSON

Give wind and tide a chance to
change.
RICHARD E. BYRD

It is a very funny thing about life:
if you refuse to accept anything
but the best you very often get it.
W. SOMERSET MAUGHAM

You can tell the ideals of a
nation by its advertisements.
NORMAN DOUGLAS

The merely well-informed man is
the most useless bore on God's
earth.
ALFRED NORTH WHITEHEAD

Unrest of spirit is a mark of life.
KARL MENNINGER

A man who reforms himself has contributed his full share towards the reformation of his neighbor.

NORMAN DOUGLAS

Prudent is he who can keep silent that part of truth which may be untimely, and by not speaking it, does not spoil the truth of what he said.

POPE JOHN XXIII

Some men see things as they are and say, why. I dream things that never were and say, why not.

ROBERT F. KENNEDY

Whenever you are asked if you can do a job, tell 'em, "Certainly I can!"—and get busy and find out how to do it.

THEODORE ROOSEVELT

The world fears a new experience
more than it fears anything.
Because a new experience
displaces so many old
experiences. . . . The world
doesn't fear a new idea. It can
pigeon-hole any idea. But it can't
pigeon-hole a real new
experience.

D. H. LAWRENCE

If you achieve success, you will
get applause, and if you get
applause, you will hear it. My
advice to you concerning
applause is this: enjoy it but
never quite believe it.

ROBERT MONTGOMERY

The optimist proclaims that we
live in the best of all possible
worlds; and the pessimist fears
this is true.

JAMES BRANCH CABELL

I am so absorbed in the wonder of earth and the life upon it that I cannot think of heaven and the angels. I have enough for this life.

PEARL BUCK

Love consists in this,
that two solitudes protect and
touch and greet each other.

RAINER MARIA RILKE

It is a wholesome and necessary
thing for us to turn again to the
earth and in the contemplation of
her beauties to know the
sense of wonder and humility.

RACHEL CARSON

There is a land of the
living and a land of the dead,
and the bridge is love.

THORNTON WILDER

Every man has to seek in his own
way to make his own self more
noble and to realize his own true
worth.

ALBERT SCHWEITZER

Life is not a spectacle or a feast;
it is a predicament.
                    GEORGE SANTAYANA

Everything science has taught me
—and continues to teach me—
strengthens my belief in the
continuity of our spiritual
existence after death. Nothing
disappears without a trace.
                    WERNHER VON BRAUN

Be nice to people on your
way up because you meet 'em
on your way down.
                    JIMMY DURANTE

It is difficult to get the news from
poems, yet men die miserably
every day for lack of what is found
there.
            WILLIAM CARLOS WILLIAMS

30

The whole of science is
nothing more than a refinement
of everyday thinking.

ALBERT EINSTEIN

To do each day two things one
dislikes is a precept I have
followed scrupulously: every day
I have got up and I have gone to
bed.

W. SOMERSET MAUGHAM

Personally I am always ready to
learn, although I do
not always like being taught.

WINSTON CHURCHILL

When a man points a finger at
someone else, he should
remember that four of his
fingers are pointing at himself.

LOUIS NIZER

It doesn't matter who you love
or how you love but that you love.
ROD McKUEN

One learns in life to keep silent
and draw one's own confusions.
CORNELIA OTIS SKINNER

What we call philosophy today
is a complicated method of
avoiding all the important
problems of life.
KENNETH REXROTH

The young man who has not
wept is a savage, and the old man
who will not laugh is a fool.
GEORGE SANTAYANA

The human race has had long
experience and a fine tradition in
surviving adversity. But we now
face a task for which we have
little experience, the task of
surviving prosperity.
ALAN GREGG

If you do not tell the truth about
yourself, you cannot
tell it about other people.

VIRGINIA WOOLF

We are possessed by the things
we possess. When I like an
object, I always give it to
someone. It isn't generosity—it's
only because I want others to be
enslaved by objects, not me.

JEAN PAUL SARTRE

To refine, to clarify, to intensify
that eternal moment in which
we alone live there is but a single
force—the imagination.

WILLIAM CARLOS WILLIAMS

The past is a work of art, full of
irrelevancies and loose ends.

MAX BEERBOHM

Older men declare war. But it is
youth that must fight and die.
And it is youth who must inherit
the tribulation, the sorrow, and
the triumphs that are the
aftermath of war.

HERBERT HOOVER

Stop the habit of wishful
thinking and start the habit of
thoughtful wishes.

MARY MARTIN

Work and love—these are the
basics. Without them there is
neurosis.

DR. THEODORE REIK

The mind is an iceberg—
it floats with only one-seventh
of its bulk above water.

SIGMUND FREUD

If there was nothing wrong
in the world there wouldn't be
anything for us to do.
GEORGE BERNARD SHAW

We can't cross a bridge until we
come to it; but I always like to lay
down a pontoon ahead of time.
BERNARD M. BARUCH

Friendship needs no words—it is
a loneliness relieved
of the anguish of loneliness.
DAG HAMMARSKJOLD

To learn to get along without, to
realize that what the world is
going to demand of us may be a
good deal more important than
what we are entitled to demand
of it—this is a hard lesson.
BRUCE CATTON

The world is round and the place
which may seem like the end may
also be only the beginning.
IVY BAKER PRIEST

You don't live in a world all alone.
Your brothers are here too.
ALBERT SCHWEITZER

The only thing that will redeem
mankind is cooperation.
BERTRAND RUSSELL

To play great music, you must
keep your eyes on a distant star.
YEHUDI MENUHIN

Each generation makes its
own accounting to its children.
ROBERT F. KENNEDY

What is moral is what you feel
good after and what is immoral is
what you feel bad after.
ERNEST HEMINGWAY

Charm is a glow within
a woman that casts a most
becoming light on others.
JOHN MASON BROWN

In literature as in love, we are
astonished at what is chosen by
others.
ANDRE MAUROIS

When a man sits with a pretty girl
for an hour, it seems like a
minute. But let him sit on a hot
stove for a minute—and it's
longer than any hour. That's
relativity.
ALBERT EINSTEIN

Hope is both the earliest and the most indispensable virtue inherent in the state of being alive. . . . If life is to be sustained hope must remain, even where confidence is wounded, trust impaired.

ERIK H. ERIKSON

Except perhaps to our God, we all have a facade, even to our closest friends; some of us even to ourselves. . . . It may not be good that we have it, but I don't believe the state or anyone else has a right to pierce that facade without the individual's consent.

MELVIN BELLI

I believe that every right implies a responsibility; every opportunity an obligation; every possession a duty.

JOHN D. ROCKEFELLER, JR.

The trouble with our age is
all signpost and no destination.
LOUIS KRONENBERGER

I have found out in later years we were very poor, but the glory of America is that we didn't know it then.

DWIGHT D. EISENHOWER

We cannot negotiate with those who say, "What's mine is mine and what's yours is negotiable."

JOHN F. KENNEDY

Baloney is the unvarnished lie laid on so thick you hate it. Blarney is flattery laid on so thin you love it.

FULTON SHEEN

The average man is more interested in a woman who is interested in him than he is in a woman with beautiful legs.

MARLENE DIETRICH

The dawn of knowledge
is usually the false dawn.

BERNARD DE VOTO

The newspapers are full of what
we would like to happen to us and
what we hope will never happen
to us.

JOHN FOWLES

Home is the place where, when
you have to go there, they have to
take you in.

ROBERT FROST

This nation, this generation, in
this hour has man's first chance to
build a Great Society, a place
where the meaning of man's life
matches the marvels of man's
labor.

LYNDON B. JOHNSON

Each honest calling, each walk of
life, has its own elite, its own
aristocracy based on excellence
of performance.

JAMES B. CONANT

Everyone is always in favor
of general economy
and particular expenditure.

ANTHONY EDEN

I have always liked bird dogs
better than kennel-fed dogs
myself—you know, one that will
get out and hunt for food rather
than sit on his fanny and yell.

CHARLES E. WILSON

To find out what one is fitted to
do and to secure an opportunity
to do it is the key to happiness.

JOHN DEWEY

Horse sense is what a horse has
that keeps him from betting
on people.

W. C. FIELDS

In war there is no second prize
for the runner-up.

OMAR BRADLEY

In the field of public education
the doctrine of "separate but
equal" has no place. Separate
educational facilities are
inherently unequal.

EARL WARREN

Things that I longed for in vain
and things that I got—let them
pass. Let me but truly possess the
things that I ever spurned and
overlooked.

RABINDRANATH TAGORE

You will do foolish things,
but do them with enthusiasm.
COLETTE

If the law is upheld only by
government officials,
then all law is at an end.
HERBERT HOOVER

It is easier to love
humanity as a whole than to
love one's neighbor.
ERIC HOFFER

Modern man worships at the
temple of science, but science
tells him only what is possible,
not what is right.
MILTON S. EISENHOWER

A general definition of
civilization: a civilized society is
exhibiting the fine qualities of
truth, beauty, adventure, art,
peace.
ALFRED NORTH WHITEHEAD

Salvation and justice are not to be
found in revolution, but
in evolution through concord.
POPE PIUS XII

Happiness makes up in height for
what it lacks in length.
ROBERT FROST

Let us never negotiate out of fear,
but let us never fear to negotiate.
JOHN F. KENNEDY

Trouble creates a capacity to
handle it.
OLIVER WENDELL HOLMES

Opinions cannot survive if one
has no chance to fight for them.
THOMAS MANN

The perfection of any matter, the
highest or the lowest, touches
on the divine.

MARTIN BUBER

Nothing in the world is so
exhilarating as to be shot at
without result.

WINSTON CHURCHILL

The story of a love is not
important—what is important is
that one is capable of love. It is
perhaps the only glimpse we are
permitted of eternity.

HELEN HAYES

I feel that the greatest reward for
doing is the opportunity to do
more.

JAMES E. SALK

Never think that war, no matter
how necessary, nor how justified,
is not a crime. Ask the infantry
and ask the dead.

ERNEST HEMINGWAY

Your success and happiness lie in
you. . . . Resolve to keep happy,
and your joy and you shall
form an invincible host against
difficulties.

HELEN KELLER

Cherish all your happy moments:
they make a fine cushion for old
age.

BOOTH TARKINGTON

Let your life lightly dance on the
edges of Time like dew on the tip
of a leaf.

RABINDRANATH TAGORE

The history of liberty has
largely been the history of the
observance of procedural
safeguards.

FELIX FRANKFURTER

The most decisive actions of our life . . . are most often unconsidered actions.

ANDRE GIDE

I accept life unconditionally. . . . Most people ask for happiness on condition. Happiness can only be felt if you don't set any condition.

ARTUR RUBINSTEIN

We need a way of life in which the animal, guided by reason, may romp but will not bite.

ABRAHAM MYERSON

Many a man wishes he were strong enough to tear a telephone book in half—especially if he has a teen-age daughter.

GUY LOMBARDO

Ask not what your country can do
for you—ask what you can
do for your country.

JOHN F. KENNEDY

There is nothing I love
as much as a good fight.

FRANKLIN DELANO ROOSEVELT

The secret of success is this:
there is no secret of success.

ELBERT HUBBARD

I don't care what is written about
me so long as it isn't true.

KATHERINE HEPBURN

Everything is funny as long as it is
happening to somebody else.

WILL ROGERS

Youth is a wonderful thing. What
a crime to waste it on children.
GEORGE BERNARD SHAW

To me, old age is always fifteen
years older than I am.
BERNARD M. BARUCH

I have never been hurt by
anything I didn't say.
CALVIN COOLIDGE

I was born a jackdaw; why
should I try to be an owl?
OGDEN NASH

Nature gives you the face you
have at twenty; it is up to you to
merit the face you have at fifty.
COCO CHANEL

On a group of theories one can found a school; but on a group of values one can found a culture, a civilization, a new way of living together among men.

IGNAZIO SILONE

Humor is an affirmation of dignity, a declaration of man's superiority to all that befalls him.

ROMAIN GARY

The question, "Who ought to be boss?" is like asking "Who ought to be the tenor in the quartet?" Obviously, the man who can sing tenor.

HENRY FORD

There are tones of voice that mean more than words.

ROBERT FROST

I have tried simply to write the
best I can; sometimes I have good
luck and write better than I can.
ERNEST HEMINGWAY

Peace and justice are two sides
of the same coin.
DWIGHT D. EISENHOWER

I am a lover and have not
found my thing to love.
SHERWOOD ANDERSON

I believe in the forgiveness of sin
and the redemption of ignorance.
ADLAI STEVENSON

Where there is an unknowable
there is a promise.
THORNTON WILDER

Never give in! Never give in!
Never, never, never, never—in
nothing great or small, large or
petty—never give in except to
convictions of honor and good
sense.

WINSTON CHURCHILL

The world today doesn't make
sense, so why should I paint
pictures that do?

PABLO PICASSO

If my husband ever met a woman
on the street who looked like
the women in his paintings, he
would faint.

MRS. PABLO PICASSO

Never grow a wishbone, daughter,
where your backbone ought to be.

CLEMENTINE PADDLEFORD

In this era of world wars, in this
atomic age, values have changed.
We have learned that we are
guests of existence, travelers
between two stations. We must
discover security within ourselves.

BORIS PASTERNAK

The best theology would need no
advocates: it would prove itself.
KARL BARTH

In war there is no substitute
for victory.
DOUGLAS MacARTHUR

We write our own destiny . . .
we become what we do.
MADAME CHIANG KAI-SHEK

Happiness is not a goal,
it is a by-product.
ELEANOR ROOSEVELT

To be able to fill leisure
intelligently is the last product of
civilization.
BERTRAND RUSSELL

In the end, art is small beer. The
really serious things are
earning one's living so as not
to be a parasite and loving one's
neighbor.

W. H. AUDEN

The pursuit of truth shall set you
free—even if you never catch up
with it.

CLARENCE DARROW

It has always seemed to me that
the most difficult part of building
a bridge would be the start.

ROBERT BENCHLEY

What is wanted is not
the will to believe but the
wish to find out, which is
its exact opposite.

BERTRAND RUSSELL

A happy marriage is a long
conversation that seems all too
short.

ANDRE MAUROIS

Art is a lie that enables us to
realize the truth.

PABLO PICASSO

The spirit of liberty is the spirit
which is not too sure that it is right.

LEARNED HAND

That's one small step for a man,
one giant leap for mankind.

NEIL ARMSTRONG

I've been rich and I've been poor;
rich is better.

SOPHIE TUCKER

Only a mediocre person is always
at his best.

W. SOMERSET MAUGHAM

History repeats itself,
and that's one of the things that's
wrong with history.

CLARENCE DARROW

You must learn day by day, year
by year, to broaden your horizon.
The more things you love, the
more you are interested in, the
more you enjoy, the more you are
indignant about—the more you
have left when anything happens.

ETHEL BARRYMORE

Life is an unanswered question,
but let's still believe in the dignity
and importance of the question.

TENNESSEE WILLIAMS

Composed in Optima, a Roman
face of graceful simplicity,
designed by Hermann Zapf.
Printed on Hallmark Eggshell
Book paper.
Set at The Castle Press,
Grant Dahlstrom, proprietor.